TYLER.
Look ye, neighbour—
You have known me long.

HOB.
Since we were boys together,
And play'd at barley-brake, and danc'd the morris:—
Some five-and-twenty years!

TYLER.
Was not I young,
And hale and happy?

HOB.
Cheerful as the best.

TYLER.
Have not I been a staid, hard-working man?
Up with the lark at labour—sober—honest—
Of an unblemish'd character?

HOB.
Who doubts it,
There's never a man in Essex bears a better.

TYLER.
And shall not these, tho' young, and hale and happy,
Look on with sorrow to the future hour?
Shall not reflection poison all their pleasures?
When I—the honest, staid, hard-working
Tyler, Toil thro' the long course of the summer's day,
Still toiling, yet still poor! when with hard labour
Scarce can I furnish out my daily food—
And age comes on to steal away my strength,
And leave me poor and wretched! Why should this be?
My youth was regular—my labour constant—
I married an industrious, virtuous woman;
Nor while I toiled and sweated at the anvil,
Sat she neglectful of her spinning wheel.
Hob—I have only six groats in the world,
And they must soon by law be taken from me.

HOB
Curse on these taxes—one succeeds another—
Our ministers—panders of a king's will—
Drain all our wealth away—waste it in revels—
And lure, or force away our boys, who should be
The props of our old age!—to fill their armies
And feed the crows of France! year follows year,
And still we madly prosecute the war;—
Draining our wealth—distressing our poor peasants—

Slaughtering our youths—and all to crown our chiefs
With Glory!—I detest the hell-sprung name.

TYLER.
What matters me who wears the crown of France?
Whether a Richard or a Charles possess it?
They reap the glory—they enjoy the spoil—
We pay—we bleed!—The sun would shine as cheerly
The rains of heaven as seasonably fall;
Tho' neither of these royal pests existed.

HOB.
Nay—as for that, we poor men should fare better!
No legal robbers then should force away
The hard-earn'd wages of our honest toil.
The Parliament for ever cries more money,
The service of the state demands more money.
Just heaven! of what service is the state?

TYLER
Oh! 'tis of vast importance! who should pay for
The luxuries and riots of the court?
Who should support the flaunting courtier's pride,
Pay for their midnight revels, their rich garments,
Did not the state enforce?—Think ye, my friend,
That I—a humble blacksmith, here at Deptford,
Would part with these six groats—earn'd by hard toil,
All that I have! To massacre the Frenchmen,
Murder as enemies men I never saw!
Did not the state compel me?
(Tax gatherers pass by)
There they go, privileg'd r——s!

(PIERS and ALICE advance to him.)

ALICE.
Did we not dance it well to-day, my father?
You know I always lov'd these village sports,
Even from my infancy, and yet methinks
I never tript along the mead so gaily.
You know they chose me queen, and your friend Piers
Wreath'd me this cowslip garland for my head—
Is it not simple?—you are sad, my father!
You should have rested from your work to-day,
And given a few hours up to merriment—
But you are so serious!

TYLER.
Serious, my good girl!
I may well be so: when I look at thee
It makes me sad! thou art too fair a flower

To bear the wintry wind of poverty!

PIERS.

Yet I have often head you speak of riches
Even with contempt: they cannot purchase peace,
Or innocence; or virtue—sounder sleep
Waits on the weary plowman's lowly bed,
Than on the downy couch of luxury
Lulls the rich slave of pride and indolence.
I never wish for wealth! My arm is strong,
And I can purchase by it a coarse meal,
And hunger savours it.

TYLER.

Young man, thy mind
Has yet to bear the hard lesson of experience.
Thou art yet young, the blasting breath of want
Has not yet froze the current of thy blood.

PIERS.

Fare not the birds well, as from spray to spray
Blithsome they bound—yet find their simple food
Scattered abundantly?

TYLER

No fancied boundaries of mine and thine
Restrain their wanderings: Nature gives enough
For all; but Man, with arrogant selfishness,
Proud of his heaps, hoards up superfluous stores
Robb'd from his weaker fellows, starves the poor,
Or gives to pity what he owes to justice!

PIERS.

So I have heard our good friend John Ball preach.

ALICE.

My father, wherefore was John Ball imprisoned?
Was he not charitable, good, and pious?
I have heard him say that all mankind are brethren,
And that like brethren they should love each other;
Was not that doctrine pious?

TYLER.

Rank sedition—
High treason, every syllable, my child!
The priests cry out on him for heresy,
The nobles all detest him as a rebel,
And this good man, this minister of Christ,
This man, the friend and brother of mankind,
Lingers in the dark dungeon!—my dear Alice,
Retire awhile.

(Exit ALICE.)

Piers, I would speak to thee
Even with a father's love! you are much with me,
And I believe do court my conversation;
Thou could'st not chuse thee forth a truer friend;
I would fain see thee happy, but I fear
Thy very virtues will destroy thy peace.
My daughter—she is young—not yet fifteen—
Piers, thou art generous, and thy youthful heart
Warm with affection; this close intimacy
Will ere long grow to love.

PIERS.
Suppose it so;
Were that an evil, Walter? She is mild
And cheerful, and industrious—now methinks
With such a partner life would be most happy!
Why would you warn me then of wretchedness?
Is there an evil that can harm our lot?
I have been told the virtuous must be happy,
And have believed it true; tell me, my friend,
What shall disturb the virtuous?

TYLER
Poverty—
A bitter foe?

PIERS.
Nay, you have often told me
That happiness does not consist in riches.

TYLER.
It is most true: but tell me, my dear boy,
Could'st thou be happy to behold thy wife
Pining with want?—the children of your loves
Clad in the squalid rags of wretchedness?
And when thy hard and unremitting toil
Had earn'd with pain a scanty recompense,
Could'st thou be patient when the law should rob thee,
And leave thee without bread and pennyless?

PIERS
It is a dreadful picture.

TYLER.
'Tis a true one.

PIERS.
But yet methinks our sober industry

Wat Tyler. A Play by Robert Southey

Robert Southey was born on the 12th of August 1774 in Bristol. A poet of the Romantic school and one of the "Lake Poets".

Although his fame has been eclipsed by that of his friends William Wordsworth and Samuel Taylor Coleridge, Southey's verse was highly influential and he wrote movingly against the horrors and injustice of the slave trade. Among his other classics are Inchcape Rock as well as a number of plays including Wat Tyler.

He was great friends with Coleridge, indeed in 1795, in a plan they soon abandoned, they thought to found a utopian commune-like society, called Pantisocracy, in the wilds of Pennsylvania.

However that same year, the two friends married sisters Sarah and Edith Fricker. Southey's marriage was successful but Coleridge's was not. In 1810 he abandoned his wife and three children to Southey's care in the Lake District. Although his income was small and those dependent upon him growing in number he continued to write and burnish his reputation with a wider public.

In 1813 on the refusal of Walter Scott he was offered by George II the post of Poet Laureate, a post Southey accepted and kept till his death 30 years later.

Southey was also a prolific letter writer, literary scholar, essay writer, historian and biographer. His biographies included those of John Bunyan, John Wesley, William Cowper, Oliver Cromwell and Horatio Nelson.

He was a renowned scholar of Portuguese and Spanish literature and history, and translated works from those two languages into English and wrote a History of Brazil (part of his planned but un-completed History of Portugal) and a History of the Peninsular War.

Perhaps his most enduring contribution is the children's classic The Story of the Three Bears, the original Goldilocks story, first published in Southey's prose collection The Doctor.

In 1838, Edith died and Southey married Caroline Anne Bowles, also a poet, on 4 June 1839

Robert Southey died on the 21st of March, 1843 and is buried in Crosthwaite Church in Keswick,

Index of Contents

ACT I.

Wat Tyler at work within. A May-pole before the Door.

ALICE, PIERS, &c.

SONG.
Cheerful on this holiday,
Welcome we the merry May.
On ev'ry sunny hillock spread,
The pale primrose rears her head;
Rich with sweets the western gale
Sweeps along the cowslip'd dale.
Every bank with violets gay,
Smiles to welcome in the May.
The linnet from the budding grove,
Chirps her vernal song of love.
The copse resounds the throstle's notes,
On each wild gale sweet music floats;
And melody from every spray,
Welcomes in the merry May.
Cheerful on this holiday,
Welcome we the merry May.

[Dance.

During the Dance, Tyler lays down his Hammer, and sits mournfully down before his Door.

[To him.

HOB CARTER.
Why so sad, neighbour?—do not these gay sports,
This revelry of youth, recall the days
When we too mingled in the revelry;
And lightly tripping in the morris dance
Welcomed the merry month?

TYLER.
Aye, we were young;
No cares had quell'd the hey-day of the blood:
We sported deftly in the April morning,
Nor mark'd the black clouds gathering o'er our noon;
Nor fear'd the storm of night.

HOB
Beshrew me, Tyler,
But my heart joys to see the imps so cheerful!
Young, hale, and happy, why should they destroy
These blessings by reflection?

Might drive away the danger, 'tis but little
That I could wish—food for our frugal meals,
Raiment, however homely, and a bed
To shield us from the night.

TYLER.
Thy honest reason
Could wish no more: but were it not most wretched
To want the coarse food for the frugal meal?
And by the orders of your merciless lord,
If you by chance were guilty of being poor,
To be turned out adrift to the bleak world,
Unhoused, unfriended?—Piers, I have not been idle,
I never ate the bread of indolence—
Could Alice be more thrifty than her mother?
Yet but with one child, and that one, how good
Thou knowest, I scarcely can provide the wants
Of nature: look at these wolves of the law,
They come to drain me of my hard earn'd wages.
I have already paid the heavy tax
Laid on the wool that clothes me—on my leather,
On all the needful articles of life!
And now three groats (and I work'd hard to earn them)
The Parliament demands—and I must pay them,
Forsooth, for liberty to wear my head.

Enter Tax-gatherers.

COLLECTOR.
Three groats a head for all your family.

PIERS.
Why is this money gathered?—'tis a hard tax
On the poor labourer!—It can never be
That government should thus distress the people.
Go to the rich for money—honest labour
Ought to enjoy its fruits.

COLLECTOR.
The state wants money.
War is expensive—'tis a glorious war,
A war of honour, and must be supported.
Three groats a head.

TYLER.
There, three for my own head,
Three for my wife's!—what will the state tax next?

COLLECTOR.
You have a daughter.

TYLER.
She is below the age—not yet fifteen.

COLLECTOR.
You would evade the tax.

TYLER.
Sir Officer,
I have paid you fairly what the law demands.

(Alice and her Mother enter the Shop. The Tax-gathers go to her. One of them lays hold of her. She screams. TYLER goes in.)

COLLECTOR.
You say she's under age.

(ALICE screams again. TYLER knocks out the Tax-gatherer's Brains. His Companions fly.

PIERS.
A just revenge.

TYLER.
Most just indeed; but in the eye of the law
'Tis murder—and the murderer's lot is mine.

(PIERS goes out.)

(TYLER sits down mournfully.)

ALICE.
Fly, my dear father! let us leave this place
Before they raise pursuit.

TYLER.
Nay, nay, my child,
Flight would be useless—I have done my duty;
I have punish'd the brute insolence of lust,
And here will wait my doom.

WIFE.
Oh let us fly!
My husband, my dear husband!

ALICE.
Quit but this place,
And we may yet be safe, and happy too.

TYLER.
It would be useless, Alice—'twould but lengthen
A wretched life in fear.

(Cry without.)
Liberty! liberty!

(Enter Mob , HOB CARTER, &c.)

(Cry) Liberty! liberty!— No Poll tax!— No War!

HOB.
We have broke our chains—we will arise in anger—
The mighty multitude shall trample down
The handful that oppress them.

TYLER
Have ye heard
So soon then of my murder?

HOB
Of your vengeance.
Piers ran throughout the village—told the news—
Cried out, to arms!—arm, arm for Liberty!
For Liberty and Justice!

TYLER
My good friends,
Heed well your danger, or be resolute;
Learn to laugh menaces and force to scorn,
Or leave me. I dare answer the bold deed—
Death must come once; return you to your homes,
Protect my wife and child, and on my grave
Write why I died; perhaps the time may come,
When honest Justice shall applaud the deed.

HOB
Nay, nay, we are oppressed, and have too long
Knelt at our proud lords' feet—we have too long
Obey'd their orders—bow'd to their caprices—
Sweated for them the wearying summer's day,
Wasted for them the wages of our toil;
Fought for them, conquer'd for them, bled for them
Still to be trampled on and still despis'd;
But we have broke our chains.

TOM MILLER.
Piers is gone on
Thro' all the neighbouring villages, to spread
The glorious tidings.

HOB
He is hurried on
To Maidstone, to deliver good John Ball,
Our friend, our shepherd.

(Mob increases.)

TYLER
Friends and Countrymen,
Will ye then rise to save an honest man
From the fierce clutches of the bloody law?
Oh do not call to mind my private wrongs,
That the state drain'd my hard-earned pittance from me;
That, of his office proud, the foul Collector
Durst with lewd hand seize on my darling child,
Insult her maiden modesty, and force
A father's hand to vengeance; heed not this:
Think not, my countrymen, on private wrongs,
Remember what yourselves have long endured.
Think of the insults, wrongs, and contumelies,
Ye bear from your proud lords—that your hard toil
Manures their fertile fields—you plow the earth,
You sow the corn, you reap the ripen'd harvest,
They riot on the produce!—That, like beasts,
They sell you with their land—claim all the fruits
Which the kindly earth produces as their own.
The privilege, forsooth, of noble birth!
On, on to Freedom; feel but your own strength,
Be but resolved, and these destructive tyrants
Shall shrink before your vengeance.

HOB
On to London—
The tidings fly before us—the court trembles—
Liberty!—Vengeance!—Justice!

END OF THE FIRST ACT

ACT II.

SCENE—BLACKHEATH.

TYLER, HOB, &c.

SONG.
' When Adam delv'd, and Eve span,
' Who was then the gentleman?'
Wretched is the infant's lot,
Born within the straw-roof'd cot!
Be he generous, wise, or brave,
He must only be a slave.
Long, long labour, little rest,
Still to toil to be oppress'd;
Drain'd by taxes of his store,

Punish'd next for being poor;
This is the poor wretch's lot,
Born within the straw-roof'd cot.
While the peasant works— to sleep;
What the peasant sows— to reap;
On the couch of ease to lie,
Rioting in revelry;
Be he villain, be he fool,
Still to hold despotic rule,
Trampling on his slaves with scorn;
This is to be nobly born.
' When Adam delv'd, and Eve span,
' Who was then the gentleman?'

JACK STRAW.
The mob are up in London— the proud courtiers
Begin to tremble.

TOM MILLER.
Aye, aye, 'tis time to tremble;
Who'll plow their fields, who'll do their drudgery now?
And work like horses, to give them the harvest?

JACK STRAW.
I only wonder we lay quiet so long.
We had always the same strength, and we deserved
The ills we met with for not using it.

HOB.
Why do we fear those animals called lords?
What is there in the name to frighten us?
Is not my arm as mighty as a Baron's?

Enter PIERS and JOHN BALL.

PIERS (to TYLER).
Have I done well, my father?— I remember'd
This good man lay in prison.

TYLER.
My dear child,
Most well; the people rise for liberty,
And their first deed should be to break the chains
That bind the virtuous:— O thou honest priest—
How much has thou endured!

JOHN BALL.
Why aye, my friend!
These squalid rags bespeak what I have suffered.
I was revil'd— insulted— left to languish
In a damp dungeon; but I bore it cheerily—

My heart was glad— for I have done my duty.
I pitied my oppressors, and I sorrowed
For the poor men of England.

TYLER.
They have felt
Their strength—look round this heath! 'tis thronged with men.
Ardent for freedom; mighty is the event
That waits their fortune.

JOHN BALL.
I would fain address them.

TYLER.
Do so, my friend, and teach to them their duty;
Remind them of their long withholden rights.
What ho there! silence!

PIERS.
Silence there, my friends,
This good man would address you.

HOB.
Aye, aye, hear him—
He is no mealy mouthed court orator,
To flatter vice, and pamper lordly pride.

JOHN BALL.
Friends! Brethren! for ye are my brethren all;
Englishmen met in arms to advocate
The cause of freedom! hear me! pause awhile
In the career of vengeance; it is true
I am a priest; but, as these rags may speak,
Not one who riots in the poor man's spoil,
Or trades with his religion. I am one
Who preach the law of Christ, and in my life,
Would practice what he taught. The son of God
Came not to you in power: humble in mien,
Lowly in heart, the man of Nazareth
Preach'd mercy, justice, love: 'Woe unto ye,
Ye that are rich:—if that ye would be saved,
Sell that ye have, and give unto the poor.'
So taught the Saviour: oh, my honest friends!
Have ye not felt the strong indignant throb
Of justice in your bosoms, to behold
The lordly Baron feasting on your spoils?
Have you not in your hearts arraign'd the lot
That gave him on the couch of luxury
To pillow his head, and pass the festive day
In sportive feasts, and ease, and revelry?
Have you not often in your conscience ask'd

Why is the difference, wherefore should that man,
No worthier than myself, thus lord it over me,
And bid me labour, and enjoy the fruits?
The God within your breasts has argued thus!
The voice of truth has murmur'd; came ye not
As helpless to the world? Shines not the sun
With equal ray on both?— Do ye not feel
The self same winds of heaven as keenly parch ye?
Abundant is the earth—the Sire of all,
Saw and pronounc'd that it was very good.
Look round: the vernal fields smile with new flowers,
The budding orchard perfumes the soft breeze,
And the green corn waves to the passing gale.
There is enough for all, but your proud Baron
Stands up, and arrogant of strength exclaims,
'I am a Lord—by nature I am noble:
These fields are mine, for I was born to them,
I was born in the castle—you, poor wretches,
Whelp'd in the cottage, are by birth my slaves.'
Almighty God! such blasphemies are utter'd!
Almighty God! such blasphemies believ'd!

TOM MILLER.
This is something like a sermon.

JACK STRAW.
Where's the bishop
Would tell you truths like these?

HOB.
There was never a bishop among all the apostles.

JOHN BALL.
My brethren!

PIERS.
Silence, the good priest speaks.

JOHN BALL.
My brethren, these are truths, and weighty ones:
Ye are all equal: nature made ye so.
Equality is your birth-right;—when I gaze
On the proud palace, and behold one man
In the blood-purpled robes of royalty,
Feasting at ease, and lording over millions,
Then turn me to the hut of poverty,
And see the wretched lab'rer worn with toil,
Divide his scanty morsel with his infants,
I sicken, and indignant at the sight,
' Blush for the patience of humanity.'

JACK STRAW.
We will assert our rights.

TOM MILLER.
We'll trample down
These insolent oppressors.

JOHN BALL.
In good truth
Ye have cause for anger: but, my honest friends,
Is it revenge or justice that ye seek?

MOB.
Justice, justice!

JOHN BALL.
Oh then remember mercy;
And though your proud oppressors spar'd not you,
Shew you excel them in humanity.
They will use every art to disunite you,
To conquer separately, by stratagem,
Whom in a mass they fear— but be ye firm—
Boldly demand your long-forgotten rights,
Your sacred, your inalienable freedom—
Be bold—be resolute—be merciful!
And while you spurn the hated name of slaves,
Shew you are men!

MOB.
Long live our honest priest!

JACK STRAW.
He shall be made archbishop.

JOHN BALL.
My brethren, I am plain John Ball, your friend,
Your equal: by the law of Christ enjoined
To serve you, not command.

JACK STRAW.
March we for London.

TYLER.
Mark me, my friends—we rise for liberty—
Justice shall be our guide: let no man dare
To plunder in the tumult.

MOB
Lead us on—
Liberty!—Justice!

(Exeunt, with cries of Liberty— no Poll Tax — no War.)

SCENE CHANGES TO THE TOWER.

KING RICHARD, ARCHBISHOP OF CANTERBURY,
SIR JOHN TRESILIAN, WALWORTH, PHILPOT.

KING
What must we do? the danger grows more imminent—
The mob increases—

PHILPOT.
Every moment brings
Fresh tidings of our peril.

KING.
It were well
To yield them what they ask.

ARCHBISHOP.
Aye, that my liege
Were politic. Go boldly forth to meet them,
Grant all they ask—however wild and ruinous—
Mean time the troops you have already summoned,
Will gather round them. Then my Christian power
Absolves you of your promise.

WALWORTH.
Were but their ringleaders cut off—the rabble
Would soon disperse.

PHILPOT.
United in a mass
There's nothing can resist them—once divide them,
And they will fall an easy sacrifice.

ARCHBISHOP.
Lull them by promises—bespeak them fair—
Go forth, my liege—spare not, if need requires,
A solemn oath, to ratify the treaty.

KING
I dread their fury.

ARCHBISHOP.
'Tis a needless dread,
There is divinity about your person;
It is the sacred privilege of Kings,
Howe'er they act, to render no account

To man. The people have been taught this lesson,
Nor can they soon forget it.

KING.
I will go—
I will submit to everything they ask;
My day of triumph will arrive at last.

(Shouts without.)
Enter Messenger.

MESSENGER.
The mob are at the city gates.

ARCHBISHOP.
Haste, haste,
Address them ere too late. I'll remain here,
For they detest me much.

(Shouts again.)
Enter another Messenger.

MESSENGER.
The Londoners have opened the city gates,
The rebels are admitted.

KING.
Fear then must give me courage; my Lord Mayor,
Come you with me.

(Exeunt. Shouts without.)

SCENE— SMITHFIELD.

WAT TYLER, JOHN BALL, PIERS, &c. Mob.

PIERS.
So far triumphant are we: how these nobles,
These petty tyrants, who so long oppress'd us,
Shrink at the first resistance!

HOB.
They were powerful
Only because we fondly thought them so.
Where is Jack Straw?

TYLER.
Jack Straw is gone to the tower
To seize the king, and so to end resistance.

JOHN BALL.
It was well judg'd: fain would I spare the shedding
Of human blood: gain we that royal puppet,
And all will follow fairly: depriv'd of him,
The nobles lose their pretext, nor will dare
Rebel against the people's majesty.

Enter Herald.

HERALD.
Richard the Second, by the grace of God,
Of England, Ireland, France, and Scotland, King,
And of the town of Berwick upon Tweed,
Would parley with Wat Tyler.

TYLER.
Let him know
Wat Tyler is in Smithfield.

(Exit Herald.)
I will parley
With this young monarch; as he comes to me
Trusting my honour, on your lives I charge you
Let none attempt to harm him.

JOHN BALL
The faith of courts
Is but a weak dependence! You are honest—
And better is it even to die the victim
Of credulous honesty, than live preserved
By the cold policy that still suspects.

Enter KING, WALWORTH, PHILPOT, &c.

KING.
I would speak to thee, Wat Tyler: bid the mob
Retire awhile.

PIERS.
Nay, do not go alone—
Let me attend you.

TYLER.
Wherefore should I fear?
Am I not arm'd with a just cause?—retire,
And I will boldly plead the cause of Freedom.

(Advances.)

KING.

Tyler, why have you kill'd my officer?
And led my honest subjects from their homes,
Thus to rebel against the Lord's anointed?

TYLER.
Because they were oppress'd.

KING.
Was this the way
To remedy the ill?— you should have tried
By milder means—petition'd at the throne—
The throne will always listen to petitions.

TYLER.
King of England,
Petitioning for pity is most weak,
The sovereign people ought to demand justice.
I kill'd your officer, for his lewd hand
Insulted a maid's modesty: your subjects
I lead to rebel against the Lord's anointed,
Because his ministers have made him odious:
His yoke is heavy, and his burden grievous.
Why do we carry on this fatal war,
To force upon the French a king they hate;
Tearing our young men from their peaceful homes;
Forcing his hard-earn'd fruits from the honest peasant;
Distressing us to desolate our neighbours?
Why is this ruinous poll tax imposed,
But to support your court's extravagance,
And your mad title to the crown of France?
Shall we sit tamely down beneath these evils
Petitioning for pity?
King of England!
Why are we sold like cattle in your markets—
Deprived of every privilege of man?
Must we lie tamely at our tyrant's feet,
And, like your spaniels, lick the hand that beats us?
You sit at ease in your gay palaces,
The costly banquet courts your appetite,
Sweet music sooths your slumbers; we the while,
Scarce by hard toil can earn a little food,
And sleep scarce shelter'd from the cold night wind:
Whilst your wild projects wrest the little from us
Which might have cheer'd the wintry hour of age:
The Parliament for ever asks more money:
We toil and sweat for money for your taxes:
Where is the benefit, what food reap we
From all the councils of your government?
Think you that we should quarrel with the French?
What boots to us your victories, your glory?
We pay, we fight, you profit at your ease.

Do you not claim the country as your own?
Do you not call the venison of the forest,
The birds of heaven your own?—prohibiting us,
Even tho' in want of food, to seize the prey
Which nature offers?—King! is all this just?
Think you we do not feel the wrongs we suffer?
The hour of retribution is at hand,
And tyrants tremble—mark me, King of England.

WALWORTH.
(Comes behind him, and stabs him.)
Insolent rebel, threatening the King!

PIERS.
Vengeance! vengeance!

HOB.
Seize the King.

KING.
I must be bold. (Advancing.)
My friends and loving subjects,
I will grant all you ask: you shall be free—
The tax shall be repeal'd— all, all you wish.
Your leader menaced me, he deserv'd his fate.
Quiet your angers; on my royal word
Your grievances shall all be done away.
Your vassalage abolish'd. A free pardon
Allow'd to all: so help me God it shall be.

JOHN BALL.
Revenge, my brethren, beseems not Christians.
Send us these terms sign'd with your seal of state.
We will await in peace: deceive us not.
Act justly, so to excuse your late foul deed.

KING.
The charter shall be drawn out: on mine honour,
All shall be justly done.

END OF ACT THE SECOND.

ACT III.

SCENE—SMITHFIELD.

PIERS (meeting JOHN BALL.)
You look disturb'd, my father?

JOHN BALL.
Piers, I am so.
Jack Straw has forced the Tower: seized the Archbishop,
And beheaded him.

PIERS.
The curse of insurrection!

JOHN BALL.
Aye, Piers! our nobles level down their vassals—
Keep them at endless labour like their brutes,
Degrading every faculty by servitude:
Repressing all the energy of the mind.
We must not wonder then, that like wild beasts,
When they have burst their chains, with brutal rage
They revenge them on their tyrants.

PIERS.
This Archbishop!
He was oppressive to his humble vassals:
Proud, haughty, avaricious.

JOHN BALL.
A true high-priest!
Preaching humility with his mitre on!
Praising up alms and Christian charity
Even whilst his unforgiving hand distress'd
His honest tenants.

PIERS.
He deserv'd his fate then.

JOHN BALL.
Justice can never link with cruelty.
Is there among the catalogue of crimes
A sin so black that only Death can expiate?
Will Reason never rouse her from her slumbers,
And darting thro' the veil her eagle eye,
See in the sable garment of the law
Revenge conceal'd? —This high priest has been haughty—
He has oppress'd his vassals: tell me, Piers,
Does his Death remedy the ills he caused?
Were it not better to repress his power
Of doing wrong—that so his future life
Might expiate the evils of the past,
And benefit mankind?

PIERS.
But must not vice
Be punished?

JOHN BALL.
Is not punishment revenge?
The momentary violence of anger
May be excus'd: the indignant heart will throb
Against oppression, and the outstretch'd arm
Resent its injured feelings: the Collector
Insulted Alice, and roused the keen emotions
Of a fond father. Tyler murder'd him.

PIERS.
Murder'd!—a most harsh word.

JOHN BALL.
Yes, murder'd him:
His mangled feelings prompted the bad act,
And Nature will almost commend the deed
That Justice blames: but will the awaken'd feelings
Plead with their heart-emoving eloquence
For the cool deliberate murder of Revenge?
Would you, Piers, in your calmer hour of reason
Condemn an erring brother to be slain?
Cut him at once from all the joys of life,
All hopes of reformation! to revenge
The deed his punishment cannot recall?
My blood boil'd in me at the fate of Tyler,
Yet I revenged not.

PIERS.
Oh my Christian father!
They would not argue thus humanely on us,
Were we within their power.

JOHN BALL.
I know they would not!
But we must pity them that they are vicious,
Not imitate their vice.

PIERS.
Alas, poor Tyler!
I do repent me much that I stood back,
When he advanced fearless in rectitude
To meet these royal assassins.

JOHN BALL.
Not for myself,
Tho' I have lost an honest virtuous friend,
Mourn I the death of Tyler: he was one
Gifted with the strong energy of mind,
Quick to perceive the right, and prompt to act
When Justice needed: he would listen to me

With due attention, yet not yielding lightly
What had to him seem'd good; severe in virtue
He awed the ruder people whom he led
By his stern rectitude.

PIERS.
Witness that day
When they destroy'd the palace of the Gaunt;
And hurl'd the wealth his avarice had amass'd,
Amid the fire: the people, fierce in zeal,
Threw in the flames the wretch whose selfish hand
Purloin'd amid the tumult.

JOHN BALL.
I lament
The death of Tyler, for my country's sake.
I shudder lest posterity enslav'd
Should rue his murder!—who shall now control
The giddy multitude, blind to their own good,
And listening with avidity to the tale
Of courtly falsehood!

PIERS.
The King must perform
His plighted promise.

(Cry without) —The Charter!—the Charter!

(Enter Mob and Herald.)

TOM MILLER.
Read it out—read it out.

HOB.
Aye, aye, let's hear the Charter.

HERALD.
Richard Plantagenet, by the grace of God,
King of England, Ireland, France, Scotland,
And the town of Berwick upon Tweed, to all
Whom it may concern, These presents,
Whereas our loving subjects have complained
To us of the heavy burdens they endure,
Particularly from our late enacted
Poll-tax; and whereas they have risen in
Arms against our officers, and demanded the
Abolition of personal slavery, vassalage, and
Manorial rights; we, ever ready in our sovereign
Mercy to listen to the petitions of our
Loving subjects, do annul all these grievances.

MOB.
Huzza! long live the king!

HERALD.
And do of our royal mercy, grant a free
Pardon to all who may have been anyways
Concerned in the late insurrections. All this
Shall be faithfully performed on our royal
Word. So help us God.
God save the King.

(Loud and repeated shouts.)

HERALD.
Now then depart in quiet to your homes.

JOHN BALL.
Nay, my good friend—the people will remain
Embodied peaceably, till Parliament
Confirm the royal charter: tell your king so:
We will await the Charter's confirmation,
Meanwhile comporting ourselves orderly
As peaceful citizens, not risen in tumult,
But to redress their evils.

Exit Herald, &c. HOB, PIERS, and JOHN BALL, remain.

HOB.
'Twas well order'd.
I place but little trust in courtly faith.

JOHN BALL.
We must remain embodied; else the king
Will plunge again in royal luxury;
And when the storm of danger is past over,
Forget his promises.

HOB.
Aye, like an aguish sinner,
He'll promise to repent when the fit's on him,
When well recover'd, laugh at his own terrors.

PIERS.
Oh ! I am grieved that we must gain so little!
Why are not all these empty ranks abolish'd;
King, slave, and lord, 'ennobl'd into MAN?'
Are we not equal all?—have you not told me
Equality is the sacred right of man,
Inalienable, tho' by force withheld?

JOHN BALL.

Even so: but Piers, my frail and fallible judgment
Knows hardly to decide if it be right,
Peaceably to return; content with little,
With this half restitution of our rights,
Or boldly to proceed through blood and slaughter,
Till we should all be equal and all happy.
I chose the milder way:—perhaps I erred.

PIERS.
I fear me—by the mass, the unsteady people
Are flocking homewards! how the multitude
Diminishes!

JOHN BALL.
Go thou, my son, and stay them.
Carter, do you exert your influence.
All depends on their stay: my mind is troubl'd,
And I would fain compose my thoughts for action.

(Exeunt HOB and PIERS.)

Father of mercies! I do fear me much
That I have err'd: thou gav'st my ardent mind
To pierce the mists of superstitious falsehood;—
Gav'st me to know the truth. I should have urg'd it
Thro' every op, perhaps,
The seemly voice of pity has deceiv'd me,
And all this mighty movement ends in ruin!
I fear me, I have been like the weak leech,
Who, sparing to cut deep, with cruel mercy
Mangles his patient without curing him.

(Great tumult.)

What means this tumult? hark! the clang of arms!
God of eternal justice! the false monarch
Has broke his plighted vow!

Enter PIERS, wounded.

PIERS.
Fly, fly, my father—the perjur'd king—fly! fly!

JOHN BALL.
Nay, nay, my child—I dare abide my fate,
Let me bind up thy wounds.

PIERS.
'Tis useless succour,
They seek thy life; fly, fly, my honour'd father.
Fain would I die in peace to hope thee safe.

I shall soon join thee, Tyler!—they are murdering
Our unsuspecting brethren: half unarm'd,
Trusting too fondly to the tyrant's vows,
They were dispersing:—the streets swim with blood.
O! save thyself.

Enter Soldiers.

SOLDIER.
This is that old seditious heretic.

(Seizes JOHN BALL.)

SECOND SOLDIER.
And here the young spawn of rebellion;
My orders ar'n't to spare him.

(Stabs PIERS.)

Come, you old stirrer-up of insurrection,
You bell-wether of the mob—you ar'n't to die
So easily.

(They lead off JOHN BALL—the tumult increases—Mob fly across the Stage—
the Troops pursue them—loud cries and shouts.)

SCENE—WESTMINSTER HALL.

KING, WALWORTH, PHILPOT, SIR JOHN TRESILIAN, &c.

WALWORTH.
My liege, 'twas wisely order'd to destroy
The dunghill rabble, but take prisoner
That old seditious priest: his strange wild notions
Of this equality, when well exposed,
Will create ridicule, and shame the people
Of their late tumults.

SIR JOHN TRESILIAN.
Aye, there's nothing like
A fair free open trial, where the king
Can chuse his jury and appoint his judges.

KING.
Walworth, I must thank you for my deliverance;
'Twas a bold deed to stab him in the parley!
Kneel down, and rise a knight, Sir William Walworth.

Enter Messenger.

MESSENGER.
I left them hotly at it. Smithfield smoked
With the rebels' blood: your troops fought loyally,
There's not a man of them will lend an ear
To pity.

SIR WILLIAM WALWORTH.
Is John Ball secur'd?

MESSENGER.
They have seiz'd him.

Enter Guards with JOHN BALL.

GUARD.
We've brought the old villain.

SECOND GUARD.
An old mischief-maker—
Why there's fifteen hundred of the mob are kill'd,
All thro' his preaching!

SIR JOHN TRESILIAN.
Prisoner! are you the arch-rebel, John Ball?

JOHN BALL.
I am John Ball; but I am not a rebel.
Take ye the name, who, arrogant in strength,
Rebel against the people's sovereignty.

SIR JOHN TRESILIAN.
John Ball, you are accus'd of stirring up
The poor deluded people to rebellion;
Not having the fear of God and of the king
Before your eyes; of preaching up strange notions
Heretical and treasonous; such as saying
That kings have not a right from heaven to govern;
That all mankind are equal; and that ranks
And the distinctions of society,
Aye, and the sacred rights of property
Are evil and oppressive:—plead you guilty
To this most heavy charge?

JOHN BALL.
If it be guilt—
To preach what you are pleas'd to call strange notions.
That all mankind as brethren must be equal;
That privileg'd orders of society
Are evil and oppressive; that the right
Of property is a juggle to deceive

The poor whom you oppress;—I plead me guilty.

SIR JOHN TRESILIAN.
It is against the custom of this court
That the prisoner should plead guilty.

JOHN BALL.
Why then put you
The needless question?—Sir Judge, let me save
The vain and empty insult of a trial.
What I have done, that I dare justify.

SIR JOHN TRESILIAN.
Did you not tell the mob they were oppress'd,
And preach upon the equality of man;
With evil intent thereby to stir them up
To tumult and rebellion?

JOHN BALL.
That I told them
That all mankind are equal, is most true:
Ye came as helpless infants to the world:
Ye feel alike the infirmities of nature;
And at last moulder into common clay.
Why then these vain distinctions!—bears not the earth
Food in abundance?—must your granaries
O'erflow with plenty, while the poor man starves?
Sir Judge, why sit you there clad in your furs?
Why are your cellars stor'd with choicest wines?
Your larders hung with dainties, while your vassal,
As virtuous, and as able too by nature,
Tho' by your selfish tyranny depriv'd
Of mind's improvement, shivers in his rags,
And starves amid the plenty he creates.
I have said this is wrong, and I repeat it—
And there will be a time when this great truth
Shall be confess'd—be felt by all mankind.
The electric truth shall run from man to man,
And the blood-cemented pyramid of greatness
Shall fall before the flash!

SIR JOHN TRESILIAN
Audacious rebel!
How darest thou insult this sacred court,
Blaspheming all the dignities of rank?
How could the Government be carried on
Without the sacred orders of the king,
And the nobility?

JOHN BALL.
Tell me, Sir Judge,

What does the government avail the peasant?
Would not he plow his field and sow the corn,
Aye, and in peace enjoy the harvest too:
Would not the sunshine and the dews descend,
Tho' neither King nor Parliament existed?
Do your Court Politics ought matter him?
Would he be warring even unto the death
With his French neighbours?—Charles and
Richard contend;
The people fight and suffer:—think ye, Sirs,
If neither country had been cursed with a chief,
The peasants would have quarrell'd?

KING.
This is treason!
The patience of the court has been insulted—
Condemn the foul mouth'd, contumacious rebel.

SIR JOHN TRESILIAN.
John Ball, whereas you are accused before us
Of stirring up the people to rebellion,
And preaching to them strange and dangerous doctrines;
And whereas your behavior to the court
Has been most insolent and contumacious;
Insulting Majesty—and since you have pleaded
Guilty to all these charges; I condemn you
To death: you shall be hanged by the neck,
But not till you are dead—your bowels opened—
Your heart torn out and burnt before your face—
Your traitorous head be sever'd from your body—
Your body quartered, and exposed upon
The city gates—a terrible example—
And the Lord God have mercy on your soul!

JOHN BALL.
Why be it so. I can smile at your vengeance,
For I am arm'd with rectitude of soul.
The truth, which all my life I have divulg'd
And am now doom'd in torment to expire for,
Shall still survive—the destin'd hour must come,
When it shall blaze with sun-surpassing splendor,
And the dark mists of prejudice and falsehood
Fade in its strong effulgence. Flattery's incense
No more shall shadow round the gore-dyed throne;
That altar of oppression, fed with rites,
More savage than the Priests of Moloch taught,
Shall be consumed amid the fire of Justice;
The ray of truth shall emanate around,
And the whole world be lighted!

KING.

Drag him hence—
Away with him to death! order the troops
Now to give quarter and make prisoners—
Let the blood-reeking sword of war be sheathed,
That the law may take vengeance on the rebels.

Robert Southey – A Concise Bibliography

The Fall of Robespierre (1794)
Joan of Arc (1796)
Icelandic Poetry, or The Edda of Sæmund (1797)
Poems (1797–1799)
Letters Written During a Short Residence in Spain and Portugal (1797)
St. Patrick's Purgatory (1798)
After Blenheim (1798)
The Devil's Thoughts (1799). Revised edition published in 1827 as "The Devil's Walk".
English Eclogues (1799)
The Old Man's Comforts and How He Gained Them (1799)
Thalaba the Destroyer (1801)
The Inchcape Rock (1802)
Madoc (1805)
Letters from England: By Don Manuel Alvarez Espriella (1807), the observations of a fictitious
Spaniard.
Chronicle of the Cid. Translated from the Spanish (1808)
The Curse of Kehama (1810)
History of Brazil (3 volumes) (1810–1819)
The Life of Horatio, Lord Viscount Nelson (1813)
Roderick the Last of the Goths (1814)
Sir Thomas Malory's Le Morte D'Arthur (1817)
Wat Tyler: A Dramatic Poem (1817)
Cataract of Lodore (1820)
The Life of Wesley; and Rise and Progress of Methodism (2 volumes) (1820)
What Are Little Boys Made Of? (1820)
The Vision of Judgement (1821)
History of the Peninsular War, 1807-1814 (3 volumes) (1823-1832)
Sir Thomas More; or, Colloquies on the Progress and Prospects of Society (1829)
The Works of William Cowper (15 vols.) (Editor) (1833-1837)
Lives of the British Admirals, with an Introductory View of the Naval History of England (5 volumes)
(1833-40); republished as "English Seamen" in 1895.
The Doctor (7 volumes) (1834-1847). Includes The Story of the Three Bears (1837).
The Poetical Works of Robert Southey, Collected by Himself (1837)

www.ingramcontent.com/pod-product-compliance
Lightning Source LLC
Chambersburg PA
CBHW060108050426
42448CB00011B/2653